D0893751

A New True Book

GERBIL PETS
AND OTHER SMALL RODENTS

By Ray Broekel

*This "true book" was prepared
under the direction of
Illa Podendorf,
formerly with the Laboratory School,
University of Chicago*

 CHILDRENS PRESS, CHICAGO

Guinea pig with her babies

PHOTO CREDITS

Root Resources — © Kitty Kohout 2; © John Kohout, Cover

Reinhard Brucker — 4, 35, 37, 41, 44 (bottom)

James Rowan — 7, 14, 27, 29 (left), 33, 42 (top), 44 (top)

Marty Hansen — 9, 13, 16, 17, 18, 23, 25, 30, 34 (2 photos), 38, 39

John Kohout — 10

Lynn M. Stone — 20, 26, 42 (bottom)

Ray Hillstrom — 29 (right), 31

Candee & Associates — 36

COVER — Gerbil

Library of Congress Cataloging in Publication Data

Broekel, Ray.
  Gerbil pets and other small rodents.

  (A New true book)
  Includes index.
  Summary: A brief introduction to the care and
feeding of pet gerbils, hamsters, guinea pigs, and mice.
    1. Rodents as pets — Juvenile literature.   [1.   Rodents
as pets.   2.   Gerbils.   3.   Hamsters.   4.   Guinea pigs.
5.   Mice as pets]   I.   Title.
SF459.R63B76   1983   636'.9323   82-23501
ISBN 0-516-01679-2   AACR2

TABLE OF CONTENTS

Baby mice drink their mother's milk.

SMALL MAMMAL PETS

Gerbils make good pets. So do hamsters, guinea pigs, and mice. They are all small mammals.

Mammals have hair on their bodies. Baby mammals take milk from their mothers.

TEETH THAT GROW

Gerbils have teeth that grow. So do hamsters, guinea pigs, and mice. These mammals are rodents.

All rodents have sharp front teeth that keep growing. So the rodents need to chew or gnaw on things. When they gnaw on something, the teeth are worn down.

WHAT ARE GERBILS?

There are many different kinds of gerbils.

The fur of a gerbil is reddish tan on the back and sides. The belly fur is white.

The body of an adult gerbil is about four inches long. Its furry tail is about as long as its body.

A pet gerbil lives for about four years.

A gerbil walks on all four legs. But it often stands up on its hind legs. When a gerbil stands up it uses its tail for balance.

A gerbil is very friendly. It is also nosy. So it often stands up just to look around.

Gerbils like
to play with
each other.

Gerbils are active day
and night. But they are
most active around midnight.

Gerbils are quiet.
Sometimes they will give
off a soft squeak. It can't
be heard more than a foot
or two away.

Gerbils will gnaw on almost anything. A piece of wood is good to chew on. Gerbils also like to dig and make tunnels.

A gerbil uses its front paws to hold onto food when eating.

GERBIL CARE

You can keep two adults and babies in a ten-gallon aquarium or a cage. They will get along well together.

When the babies grow up, move some of them to another home. Only keep about four adults together. That way there will be plenty of room.

Gerbils don't like it too hot or too cold. Keep their home in a room where you are comfortable.

Put about an inch of litter on the floor of their home. Wood shavings make good litter.

Change the litter when it gets messy. Take out spoiled food, too. Gerbils are clean. They like to live where it is clean.

Give your gerbils a few clean rags or empty toilet paper rolls. The gerbils will make nests out of the rags or paper.

Gerbils need exercise. So a run on a wheel is good for them.

Gerbils like to play with toys.
This plastic boot is a good gerbil toy.

Gerbils like to eat sunflower seeds.

Gerbils don't overeat. So don't give them more food than they will eat in one day. Extra food will spoil.

Use a small dish for food. Give them some food pellets each day. Food can be bought at pet stores.

Feed your gerbil a lettuce leaf four times a week. It will also eat pieces of carrot, cabbage, and celery. Don't give it too much fresh food or it might get sick.

Gerbils use up most of the food they eat. So gerbils give off little waste matter.

Gerbils will drink from a water bottle.
They drink standing up on their hind legs.

Gerbils get most of their water from their food. But it is a good idea to give them a water bottle, too.

When holding a gerbil, don't squeeze it.

A gerbil is gentle, but it can bite and scratch. So never hold it close to your face.

One way to pick up a gerbil is to place your hand inside its home. The gerbil should crawl onto your hand. Then you can lift it.

Here is another way to pick up a gerbil. Grasp it firmly by the base of the tail. Slowly lift it up with its head down. Then lower it onto your other hand.

Baby gerbils are called pups. A group of pups is called a litter. There are about five pups in a litter.

The pups cannot see and have no hair when born. They are a bright pink in color.

They drink milk from their mother until they are about twenty days old. By then they can see, have hair, and can be handled safely.

WHAT ARE HAMSTERS?

Hamsters come in different colors.

Hamsters are about six inches long. Their tails are about half an inch long.

A hamster's legs are short. So a hamster waddles when it walks.

Angora hamster

About seven babies are born in a litter. They are born naked and blind.

They will have fur and be able to see in about three weeks.

Hamsters don't overeat. And they don't waste food. If they find extra food, they will keep it to eat later.

Hamsters have pouches in their cheeks. They can store a lot of food in their pouches.

HAMSTER CARE

A cage with a sliding bottom tray makes a good hamster home. Newspapers can be used to cover the cage floor.

A feeding dish and a water bottle are needed. Both should be fastened to the side of the cage. That way the hamster won't knock them over.

Take good care of your pet.

Hamsters will keep food in their cheek pouches.

Clean the hamster cage at least once a week.

A hamster also needs to exercise. So an exercise wheel is needed.

A hamster's teeth grow. So give it a beef or ham bone to chew. A piece of hardwood works well, too.

You can buy hamster food pellets at most pet stores. Put some pellets in the food dish each day.

Feed a hamster fresh fruits and vegetables about once a week.

You can give the hamster a lettuce or cabbage leaf. A carrot, grape, or a piece of fresh apple can be given, too.

Hamsters like to move around at night.

They should be kept out of sunlight during the day.

Keep them out of drafts.
Then they won't catch
cold.

When they are eight
weeks old, hamsters start
to fight with each other. So
it is best to keep just one
in a cage.

A hamster lives well by itself. It doesn't get lonely.

A hamster can be picked up carefully if it is cupped in the hands.

A hamster can be picked up by the scruff of its neck, too.

A hamster may bite you, so be careful with it.

WHAT ARE GUINEA PIGS?

Guinea pigs are small rodents like gerbils and hamsters. Another name for the guinea pig is cavy.

Adult guinea pigs are from eight to ten inches long.

They have hair that can be long or short, smooth or rough. The colors are brown, black, white, tan, or mixed colors.

Guinea pigs have no tails.

They have short legs.

They can live to be seven or eight years old.

There may be from five to twelve guinea pig babies in a litter.

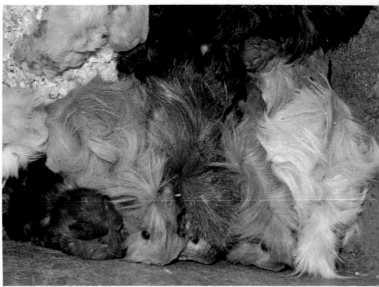

Guinea pigs can have long hair (above) or short hair (left). They do not fight with each other and can live together in large groups.

Guinea pigs sometimes squeal, grunt, or whistle. Their voices are not loud.

Guinea pigs sleep at night. They are busy during the day.

Guinea pigs will drink from water bottles.

GUINEA PIG CARE

A twenty-gallon aquarium makes a good home for one large or two small guinea pigs.

Guinea pigs don't fight each other. They get along well.

Hay, wood shavings, or newspapers make good litter, or bedding.

Keep the bedding clean. Change it before it begins to smell.

A guinea pig likes a place to be by itself every now and then. So put a small cardboard box inside the home.

Guinea pigs should be kept where it is warm.

Guinea pigs don't need an exercise wheel or other toys on which to exercise and play.

Guinea pigs need both dry and fresh food every day. Pellet food made for rabbits is a very good dry food.

Guinea pigs will also eat
hay and fresh food such
as apples, carrots, and
lettuce. They also eat fresh
grass and cauliflower leaves.

Guinea pigs do not
overeat. So find out how
much fresh food and water
will be eaten in a day.
Then you will not overfeed.

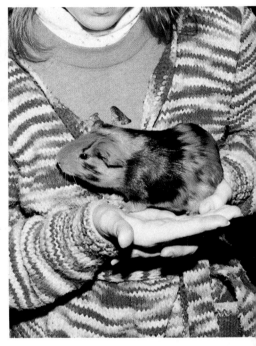

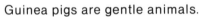
Guinea pigs are gentle animals.

Guinea pigs are gentle.
Be sure to pick them up
carefully so you don't hurt
them.

WHAT ARE MICE?

Mice have furry bodies. Their tails have no hair on them.

Many pet mice are white. Others are black, tan, and a mix of colors. There are about seventy shades of color in all.

Baby mice are born blind and without hair.

Mice can have lots of babies. There are about seven babies in a litter. Some mice may have as many as fifteen litters in just one year.

MOUSE CARE

Mice are clean animals. They will almost always use the same spot as the bathroom.

Sawdust or shredded newspaper is good to use on the bottom of the cage. Keep the litter clean. Your nose will tell you when it needs changing.

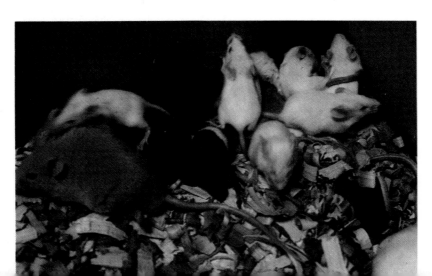

The best way to pick up
a mouse is by the tail.
Hold it firmly at the middle
of the tail, not by the tip.
Then place the mouse in
the palm of your other hand.

Mice like to play on an exercise wheel.

Mice like to move around. They will play on exercise wheels, ladders, and other toys.

A mother mouse wants to make a nest for her babies. She can use cotton or soft paper, such as paper towels.

Some good dry foods for mice are rabbit pellets, oats, bird seed, and dog biscuits.

Mice eat fresh carrots, dandelion leaves, and flowers, too.

Give your mice fresh water, too.

Mice will drink from a hanging water bottle.

Take out any uneaten fresh food before it spoils. Mice need things to gnaw on. Acorns or walnuts are good for this. So are small beef bones.

Gerbil

Angora hamster

THEY ARE IN YOUR CARE

Gerbils and hamsters
make good pets. So do
guinea pigs and mice.
They will give you many
hours of fun as you watch
them or play with them.

Guinea pig

White mouse

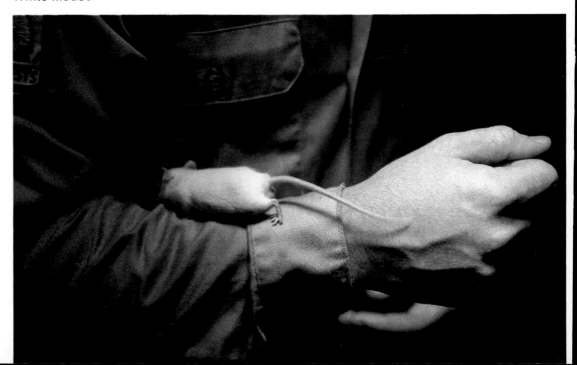

Your pets depend on you. They look to you for fresh food and water. You must keep their homes clean and dry. They are in your care. So do your part to keep them healthy.

About the Author

*Ray Broekel is well known in the publishing field as a teacher,
editor, and author of science materials for young people. A full-time
freelance writer, Dr. Broekel also writes many other kinds of books
for both young people and adults. He has had over 130 published.
His first book was published by Childrens Press in 1956. Ray
Broekel lives with his wife, Peg, and a dog, Fergus, in Ipswich,
Massachusetts.*